IØ151657

"The theological world tends to be very prosaic, so it is refreshing to read the poetry of a faithful Christian hymnist whose craft is informed by biblical truth rather than maudlin sentimentality. I know from personal experience that Justin Wainscott weaves the great hymns of the faith into his preaching each week. And I know that if you prick him, he will bleed the language of those hymns. Having had the privilege of singing some of my pastor's hymns in worship, it's a special delight to have this collection for devotional reading and singing. I also commend them to the churches for public worship."

—C. BEN MITCHELL

Graves Professor of Moral Philosophy, Union University

"Moses taught the delivered children of Israel a song. David entrusted Asaph with a psalm of thanksgiving to the Lord. Ambrose shared his hymns. Luther followed 'the example of the prophets and ancient fathers of the church,' writing songs and urging others to do the same. Likewise, Calvin, Watts, Newton, and Spurgeon all contributed to the deep stream of poetry that continues to edify the church and proclaim the gospel. Today, as much as before, we need great pastors and theologians, leaders of God's people, to capture our language and bring it into the service of our King. More than ditties that elevate our pulse, we need biblical truths artistically expressed that quicken our minds, prick our hearts, and order our loves. I am deeply grateful for Justin Wainscott, a dedicated lover of God's Word and God's People, for heeding this call, penning these words, and courageously offering them for our benefit. May he write more and may his writing spur others to do the same."

—CHRISTOPHER MATHEWS

Dean of the College of Fine Arts, Oklahoma Baptist University

"In a world filled with the immediacy of information and entertainment, we often overlook the opportunity for quiet moments of reflection, meditation, and prayer. Wainscott's hymns stand in a rich theological tradition of pastor hymn-writing and cause us to slow down, marveling at the gift of creation, Christ, and his redemption. Through lyric and poetry, Wainscott recaptures a sense of wonder at nature, relationships, grace, and ultimately, union with the Divine encountered through worship."

—AUTUMN ALCOTT RIDENOUR

Assistant Professor, Religious and Theological Studies, Merrimack College

"For much of Christian history, pastors and preachers were instrumental in expressing and shaping Christian faith by composing hymns and poetry. From Watts to Wesley, Luther to Lowry, pastors penned their reflections on biblical truth and their personal expressions of authentic Christian faith. Pastor Justin Wainscott's *Lost in Wonder, Love, and Praise* is a refreshing return to this rich heritage. His compilation brings together years of his own hymns, poetry, and theological musings. They are rich yet readable— instructional and devotional. Above all, they are biblical, Christ-centered, and saturated with the gospel. For several years, I have been blessed and encouraged by reading the hymns and poetry of Justin Wainscott. I am so pleased that these words are now available in a single collection so others may be refreshed as well. I highly recommend this resource to pastors, worship leaders, and laypersons alike."

—SCOTT SHEPHERD

Music and Worship Specialist, Tennessee Baptist Mission Board

Lost in Wonder, Love, and Praise

"Justin Wainscott is a rarity—a faithful biblical expositor with superb pastoral gifts who is also a skilled poet and an excellent hymn writer. Here we have some of his best work offered to the church and meant to bless the Lord's people everywhere. A book of spiritual reading for morning and evening in every season of life."

—TIMOTHY GEORGE

Founding Dean of Beeson Divinity School of Samford University and General Editor of the Reformation Commentary on Scripture

"Majestic and meaningful, edifying and enabling, creative and contemplative, the beautiful hymns and poems found in *Lost in Wonder, Love, and Praise* will provide a wonderful resource for followers of Jesus Christ. The hymns and poems connect with key days on the calendar of the church and with the many events and challenges that characterize life. Readers will be encouraged and strengthened in their spiritual journeys as well as in their worship of the one true, and living God. Seekers will find a source to guide them to the grace of the Lord Jesus Christ. The hymns and poems are both artistically inviting and theologically sound, bringing glory to the Trinitarian God. The book is a marvelous worship resource that will without doubt serve as a source of strength, devotion, and enablement for those who take time to reflect on these creative pieces. It is both a joy and a privilege to recommend this work from Justin Wainscott."

—DAVID S. DOCKERY

President, Trinity Evangelical Divinity School

"Justin Wainscott has provided the hymns and poetry our souls can sing as we consider the greatness of our God and are *Lost in Wonder, Love, and Praise*. Writing of spiritual and mundane experiences viewed through the lenses of wonder and love, Wainscott leads us to praise our Triune God from whom all blessings flow with theology that sings. If you want to be ushered in to the sacred place—both corporately and individually—open your heart to this great theo-musicological work."

—ROBERT SMITH, JR.

Charles T. Carter Baptist Chair of Divinity, Beeson Divinity School

"In days gone by, pastors were quite commonly poets and the authors of many of our great hymns. The loss of poetry among our pastors has been detrimental in many ways. Justin Wainscott, in this wonderful collection of original poems, demonstrates a return to these old paths. Pastors, notice how the careful and beautiful use of words can help you reach the heart. Believers, in general, experience how slowly contemplating these poetic meditations can nurture your soul, lead you in praise, give words for your laments, and generally tune your heart to God. This has been my experience as I have read these poems, and as we have sung many of them in church. I heartily commend this volume to you, confident it will be a blessing."

—RAY VAN NESTE

Dean of the School of Theology and Missions, Union University

"I love that Justin Wainscott is following in the footsteps of Charles Wesley and John Newton as a hymn-writing pastor. His hymns and poems flow out of the wrestling done in a pastor's study to communicate God's Word to his people. These cross-focused hymns are both sound and singable, and will bless many individuals and congregations."

—BETSY HOWARD

Author of Seasons of Waiting *and editor at The Gospel Coalition*

"Theology is art as much as it is science. This is especially true when the glory of our Triune God in his works of creation and redemption are celebrated through the medium of poetry. My friend and former pastor Justin Wainscott is a contemporary pastor-poet-theologian whom God has gifted to set sacred truths to moving verse. In doing so, Justin takes upon himself the mantle of Wesley and Dutton, of Rossetti and Donne, of Hopkins and Bradstreet. Whether his hymns and poems endure for centuries like the works of these great artist-theologians is a matter left to God's providence. But for such a time as this, his poems and hymns are a gift to the church. Take up and read."

—NATHAN A. FINN

Provost and Dean of the University Faculty, North Greenville University, Tigerville, SC

Lost in Wonder, Love, and Praise

Hymns & Poems

JUSTIN WAINSCOTT

RESOURCE *Publications* · Eugene, Oregon

LOST IN WONDER, LOVE, AND PRAISE
Hymns & Poems

Copyright © 2019 Justin Wainscott. All rights reserved. Except for brief quotations in critical publications or reviews, no part of this book may be reproduced in any manner without prior written permission from the publisher. Write: Permissions, Wipf and Stock Publishers, 199 W. 8th Ave., Suite 3, Eugene, OR 97401.

Resource Publications
An Imprint of Wipf and Stock Publishers
199 W. 8th Ave., Suite 3
Eugene, OR 97401

www.wipfandstock.com

PAPERBACK ISBN: 978-1-5326-7972-8
HARDCOVER ISBN: 978-1-5326-7973-5
EBOOK ISBN: 978-1-5326-7974-2

Manufactured in the U.S.A.   MARCH 14, 2019

"A Warning to My Readers," Copyright © 1987 by Wendell Berry, from *Collected Poems (1957-1982)*. Reprinted by permission of Counterpoint Press.

Scripture quotations are from the ESV® Bible (The Holy Bible, English Standard Version®), copyright © 2001 by Crossway, a publishing ministry of Good News Publishers. Used by permission. All rights reserved.

For Anna,
who has "the imperishable beauty of a gentle and quiet spirit,
which in God's sight is very precious" (1 Peter 3:4).

And for Ella, Graham, and Gavin,
my "heritage from the Lord" (Psalm 127:3).

Contents

Preface

A Note to My Readers

I UNDERSTAND IF YOU'RE wondering why a pastor would write a book of poetry, or if you're wondering whether the words *pastor* and *poet* even belong together. I admit, it took me years to see the connection.

For much of my early church-going life, I held hymnbooks in my hands and sang the words written there without ever paying attention to the small print at the bottom of its pages. I failed to notice that there were names included in the hymnal, names of the hymn writers and names of the musicians who composed the tunes.

But something happened while I was in seminary. I actually began to pay attention to the small print at the bottom of the pages. And to my surprise, I began to notice that some of the names of the pastors and theologians I was reading from church history were the same names that appeared in the hymnbook. Names like Martin Luther, Isaac Watts, John Newton, and Charles Wesley. I knew these men as pastors and preachers, but not as poets and hymn writers.

I can't quite explain how or why, but that newfound revelation that these pastors were also poets had a profound effect on me. I began to wonder why this legacy was seemingly lost in our own day, why more pastors weren't writing hymns and poems. Before long, my curiosity grew into fascination, and my fascination turned into an invitation to try my hand at joining this long line of pastor-poets. And thus began my first attempts at writing poetry, a practice I have continued ever since. While my work may fall far short of the likes of Watts and Wesley and Newton, I'm at least attempting to keep good company. And the book you now hold in your hands contains some of those attempts. It is a collection of both hymns and poems, written over the course of several years.

Now, because this is a book of poetry and because we don't currently read poetry in our culture as much as we do prose (and because many people don't read much poetry at all), I thought it might prove beneficial here at the outset to provide you with a few tips about how best to engage with poetry. *First, read poetry out loud.* You need to hear the sounds—the assonance, the alliteration, the rhyming patterns—and you need to feel something of the verbal cadence to get the full effect. *Second, read poetry slowly and carefully.* Poetry is not meant to be skimmed. It's not meant to be read the way you read an online article or the way you scan social media. It requires a different kind of reading. Meditate on each line, paying close attention to the words and to the imagery. *Third, read it again.* Don't settle for only reading a poem once. Read it at least two or three times.

I also want to offer a few tips about engaging with the hymns in this book. I know we think of hymns as songs to be sung, which is true. But remember that hymns are also lyrical poems. So I encourage you simply to read the hymns first. Just read and reflect on the words. Then, you can go back and sing them (you will notice that for most of the hymns, I have suggested a familiar tune so that you can easily sing them—whether by yourself, with your family, or even with your church). And for those of you who are musicians, feel free to sing them to other tunes that fit the meter or even to compose new tunes for them.

The poetry in this book is written primarily with Christian readers in mind and will probably serve best as a devotional resource, something to read alongside the Bible. Its aim is not to compete with your reading of the Scriptures but to accompany it, to help you reflect on the truths of God's Word and God's world so that you too might get "lost in wonder, love, and praise." But if you are not a Christian, I hope you will still read and benefit from this book. Indeed, I would be delighted if in reading it you came to put your faith in the loving, gracious Savior whose poetic praise fills much of the following pages.

If you find that there are hymns, poems, or phrases that you enjoy, I would remind you of words from the poet Wendell Berry, which certainly apply here too:

Do not think me gentle
because I speak in praise
of gentleness, or elegant
because I honor the grace
that keeps this world. I am
a man crude as any,
gross of speech, intolerant,
stubborn, angry, full
of fits and furies. That I
may have spoken well
at times, is not natural.
A wonder is what it is.

A wonder, indeed!

Justin Wainscott
Epiphany 2019

Acknowledgments

I AM SINCERELY GRATEFUL for all those who have played a part in the book you now hold in your hands. To the faculty of Beeson Divinity School, thank you for opening my eyes to the rich history of pastor-poets. To the churches I have been privileged to serve—First Baptist Somerville, Pleasant Plains Baptist, First Baptist Paducah, and First Baptist Jackson—thank you for allowing me to use your church newsletters as an initial space for my poetry and thank you for the joy of hearing my hymns sung in your gathered worship (the members of First Baptist Jackson have been particularly encouraging and affirming in this regard). To my fellow pastors, with whom I have the privilege of serving, thank you for being such faithful and joyful co-laborers. To the friends and colleagues who have shown interest and appreciation in my work, your comments mean more than you know. To everyone at Wipf and Stock, and especially Matt Wimer, thank you for your help in every step of this journey and for taking a chance on a first-time author. To Jeff Thompson, thank you for lending your artistic gifts to design the cover. Though I am not a musician, I have been blessed by a number of friends who are, and the conversations and collaborations I have had with them over the years has enriched my thinking and my writing. They include Ron Boud, Chris Mathews, Phil McKibben, Steve Moore, Scott Shepherd, Zach Young, and two who have now joined the great cloud of witnesses, Paul Clark and Dan Musselman. I am also indebted to the mentors, friends, and colleagues who added their kind endorsements to this book. Without the consistent encouragement and gentle nudging of one of those friends, Ray Van Neste, this book would likely not exist. My parents, Mike and Rose, have been extremely supportive of this endeavor, just as they have been throughout my life. My children have been a joy (and have inspired me on more than one occasion). And my dear wife, Anna, who inspired my very first poem, has enriched my life in so many ways and has loved me so much better than I deserve. For all these who have played a part in making this book a reality, I say, "Thanks be to God."

Hymns

Blest Is the One Who Does Not Walk (Psalm 1)

Blest is the one who does not walk
In schemes of wicked men,
Nor stands amid the sinners' way,
Nor joins the scoffers' den.
But in God's true and perfect law
He places his delight;
And on that law he meditates
Both ev'ry day and night.

For he is nourished like a tree
That's planted by a stream,
That in due season yields its fruit,
Whose leaf is always green.
But lo, the wicked are not so;
No fruit do they display.
But they, instead, are like the chaff
The wind just drives away.

Therefore the wicked will not stand
When judgment does befall;
Nor sinners join that righteous throng
In Glory's sacred hall.
But God, the Lord and Judge, does know
The righteous and their way;
In Christ they're hid, while wicked men
Will perish on that day.

Can be sung to the tune of "I Sing the Mighty Power of God" (FOREST GREEN) or "It Came Upon a Midnight Clear" (CAROL) or "My Shepherd Will Supply My Need" (RESIGNATION)

O Lord, How Many Are My Foes (Psalm 3)

O Lord, how many are my foes,
How vast my enemy;
Their vicious taunts, like deadly blows,
Suggest You'll not save me.

But Lord, You are to me a shield;
You heard me when I cried.
Pray'r was the weapon I did wield,
And help You soon supplied.

So I lay down, sustained by You,
And slept in perfect peace.
I woke, a thousand foes in view,
Yet all my fears had ceased.

Arise, O Lord; deliver me;
Salvation comes from You.
O Jesus, crush the enemy,
And bless Your people too.

Can be sung to the tune of "Amazing Grace" (NEW BRITAIN) or "O God, Our Help in Ages Past" (ST. ANNE)

Be Gracious Unto Us, O God (Psalm 67)

*For a Missionary Commissioning Service at
First Baptist Church, Jackson, Tennessee*

Be gracious unto us, O God,
O let Your blessings flow.
And make Your face to shine on us;
Your favor, Lord, bestow,
That all Your ways, salvation too,
Might on the earth be known,
And all the nations worship You
As God, and God alone.

O fill the peoples with Your praise,
All peoples of the earth;
And let them sing Your saving ways,
Your wonders and Your worth.
O fill the peoples with Your praise,
All nations, tribes, and tongues;
And let them laud the God who saves
In glad and joyful songs.

O bless us, God, that we might be
A blessing to the world,
So that the nations come to see
And fear You as the Lord.
O send us out in Jesus' name,
Yes, send us 'cross the waves;
Till peoples everywhere proclaim
The truth that Jesus saves!

*Can be sung to the tune of "I Sing the Mighty Power of God" (FOREST
GREEN)*

All Nations, Praise the LORD (Psalm 117)

All nations, praise the LORD!
All peoples, Him extol!
Let praise be heard around the world,
And joy from pole to pole.

O praise Him for His love,
T'ward us, whom He adores.
And praise our God, who reigns above;
He's faithful evermore.

O praise Him! Praise the LORD!
All tribes and tongues confess
That Jesus Christ alone is Lord,
And shall be ever blest!

Can be sung to the tune of "Blest Be the Tie" (DENNIS)

Out of the Depths I Raise My Cry (Psalm 130)

Out of the depths I raise my cry;
Lord, hear my weary plea.
Incline Your ear from heav'n on high;
Show mercy unto me.

If You, O Lord, should mark our sins,
There'd be no hiding place;
But You forgive and don't condemn.
We marvel at Your grace.

My waiting soul in hope is drawn
To His unchanging Word;
And more than watchmen for the dawn,
My soul waits for the Lord.

O let us place our hope in God,
And sound this grateful theme:
From ev'ry sin, our Savior's blood
Will lovingly redeem.

Can be sung to the tune of "Amazing Grace" (NEW BRITAIN) or "Must Jesus Bear the Cross Alone" (MAITLAND)

O Lord, My Heart's Not Lifted Up (Psalm 131)

O Lord, my heart's not lifted up;
My eyes aren't raised too high.
With things too great and marvelous,
I am not occupied.

I've learned to calm my fretful soul,
And hush my clam'ring fears;
My soul is like a weaned, young child,
Content his mother's near.

So in the Lord let all the hope
Of God's redeemed now be;
From this time forth and evermore,
Through all eternity.

Can be sung to the tune of "O God, Our Help in Ages Past" (ST. ANNE)

Praise to God, the Three in One

Before the world was e'er designed,
Or time had yet begun,
'Twas perfect fellowship divine
Between the Three in One.
In lack of nothing, needing naught,
Yet moved by grace alone,
Redemption's plan the Godhead wrought
To make His glory known.

Yea, long before creation's days
Or man ate of the tree,
God had ordained for Triune praise
Salvation, full and free.
So praise to God, the Three in One,
Who 'fore the fall decreed
The saving mission of the Son
To undo Adam's deed.

In time pre-set, the Three in One
Fulfilled the fixed decree:
The Father sent the'ternal Son
To die on Calvary;
Then sent His Spirit to our hearts,
The Spirit from on high,
And all the blessings Christ imparts,
The Spirit does apply.

So praise to God, the Three in One,
For setting sinners free;
The curse of sin is now undone,
Sweet, Triune victory.

O Father, Spirit, Son, to Thee,
The Holy Trinity,
All glory, laud, and honor be
Throughout eternity.

Can be sung to the tune of "Blessed Be the God of Israel" (FOREST GREEN)

Sing Highest Praises to Our King

Advent/Christmas Hymn

Sing highest praises to our King,
Who left His throne above;
And clothed Himself in flesh to bring
The blessings of His love.

The glory He had long enjoyed,
He humbly set aside;
How great the means which Christ employed
To save a sinful Bride!

In Bethlehem by virgin birth,
As prophets did foretell;
Our God descended to the earth,
And didst among us dwell.

We see Him in the manger lay,
But let us ne'er forget;
This precious Child was born to pay
Our cursed, sinful debt.

This perfect Lamb for sinners slain,
Who died and rose again,
Now sits on David's throne and reigns
In vict'ry over sin.

So let our longing hearts all burn
With zeal for Christ our King,
And for the day of His return,
When He shall reign supreme!

Can be sung to the tune of "O for a Thousand Tongues" (AZMON)

Immortal God in Mortal Flesh

Advent/Christmas Hymn

Immortal God in mortal flesh,
Our Lord has come to earth;
Incarnate God, He came to bring
The gift of second birth.

Spread gospel tidings all around.
Let sinners celebrate!
For Christ was born to save us all
From sin's condemning fate.

In mercy God has sent His Son
To bear the curse of sin;
To hang condemned on Calv'ry's cross,
And pardon sinful men.

This precious babe of Bethlehem
Will be forever blessed;
He ransomed us from hell's domain
To enter heaven's rest.

So to our great Immanuel,
Glad songs of praise we'll sing;
From now and through eternity,
He'll reign, our saving King.

*Can be sung to the tune of "O God, Our Help in Ages Past" (ST. ANNE) or
"Am I a Soldier of the Cross" (ARLINGTON)*

All People of the Coming King

Advent/Christmas Hymn

All people of the coming King,
All servants of the Lord,
Come lift your voices, let us sing
With hearts in one accord:
Alleluia! Alleluia!

In Bethlehem the angels praised
The birth of Christ our King;
So let us now with voices raised
Rejoice with them and sing:
Alleluia! Alleluia!

Oh, marvel in the mystery
Of Jesus' virgin birth;
To God all praise and glory be,
And peace o'er all the earth.
Alleluia! Alleluia!

His first advent salvation wrought
By dying on the tree;
Yet He, through resurrection, bought
For us eternity.
Alleluia! Alleluia!

To Him who came and conquered sin,
Triumphant and supreme;
To Him who'll one day come again,
We sound this joyous theme:
Alleluia! Alleluia!

And when He comes, our King, to reign,
And earth and heav'n be new;
Then may the sound of this refrain
Our longing hearts renew:
Alleluia! Alleluia!

O Jesus Christ, Our King and Priest

O Jesus Christ, our King and Priest,
Melchizedek's true line;
Although with us God now is pleased,
The work was wholly Thine.

The debt of sin required a price
Your blood has fully paid;
In Your great priestly sacrifice,
Atonement has been made.

With voices strong we sing these notes
Of mercy's cleansing flood;
No more the need for bulls and goats,
Sufficient is Your blood!

Your offering was once for all,
Yet lasts forevermore;
Our risen Lamb reversed the fall,
And opened heaven's door.

And now for us You intercede,
Our great High Priest on high;
For ransomed sinners You do plead,
And offer up Your cry.

With full assurance we can trust
Your ev'ry plea is heard;
The Father shall, indeed, He must
Accept Your ev'ry word.

So give us confidence to know
Our hope's secure in Thee;
And let Your priestly blessings flow
Through all eternity.

Can be sung to the tune of "All Hail the Power of Jesus' Name" (CORONATION)

Christ's Atoning Wounds

In honor of the faculty of Beeson Divinity School

That sacred stream which ever flows,
Flows from the Savior's wounds,
Does in the souls of saints compose
Sweet Christ-exalting tunes.

So let the saints in chorus flood
This place with songs of praise;
And sing of Christ's redeeming blood,
And marvel at His grace.

The precious wounds of Christ above—
His hands, His feet, His side—
Stand as a witness to His love
For us, His ransomed Bride.

Those wounds which paid our sinful debt
Remove all grounds for pride;
For God's requirements all were met
When Christ our Savior died.

So let us boast in Him alone,
And in the wounds He bears;
Since He who sits on heaven's throne
Those sacred scars still wears.

And when before that throne we stand
And on our Savior gaze,
We'll truly come to understand
His wounds deserve our praise.

Can be sung to the tune of "O for a Thousand Tongues" (AZMON) or "Alas, and Did My Savior Bleed" (AVON)

How Slow and Dull of Heart Are We

How slow and dull of heart are we,
Held fast by sin's dread sway;
That we would gaze on Calv'ry's tree,
And want to look away.
But oh! how beautiful the sight
Of sin in gross defeat;
Of darkness bowing to the Light,
And victory complete!

How feebly do our souls believe
The gospel's saving grace;
That Christ would all God's wrath receive,
And suffer in our place.
But oh! how wonderful the thought
Of pardon full and free;
Of knowing that by Christ we're bought,
And His we'll ever be!

How little do our minds perceive
The depths of what it cost
For Christ our Savior to relieve
Our burden on the cross.
But oh! how glorious the plan
That saved our wretched race;
Conceived before the world began,
Secured by sov'reign grace!

How weakly do our praises ring,
Cause we've not understood
That all-sufficient mercy springs
From Christ's atoning blood.

But oh! the day when we shall know
In full and not in part,
The saving pow'r His blood bestows
On ev'ry ransomed heart!

Can be sung to the tune of "It Came Upon a Midnight Clear" (CAROL) or "My Shepherd Will Supply My Need" (RESIGNATION)

Jesus Is Risen, He's Risen Indeed

Easter/Resurrection Hymn

Jesus is risen, He's risen indeed;
Granting new life to all Abraham's seed.
Death's been defeated for those He doth save;
Jesus, our Victor, has conquered the grave.

No more dominion for death, hell, and sin;
Ours is the vict'ry that Jesus did win.
Let us stand firm, then, for our Lord does reign,
Knowing our labors are never in vain.

O ransomed sinners, together proclaim
That name exalted above ev'ry name:
Jesus our Savior, now raised from the dead,
Reigning forever, our glorious Head.

Our hope's unshaken, in which we now stand.
Christ is alive at the Father's right hand,
From whence He's coming again for His own.
Hasten the day, Lord, and carry us home.

Can be sung to the tune of "Be Thou My Vision" (SLANE)

To Jesus Christ, Our Living Lord

Easter/Resurrection Hymn

To Jesus Christ, our living Lord,
This grateful song we bring;
For He has conquered sin and hell,
Removed death's awful sting!

With steadfast hope and boundless joy,
We celebrate today;
The bonds of death are broken all,
The stone's been rolled away!

Death's hostile hold could not contain
His power o'er the grave;
Christ rose again in victory,
Our wretched souls to save!

No longer slaves to fear and death,
Triumphant let us be;
The victory that Christ has won,
He won for you and me!

Though death's the final enemy,
Its end is drawing nigh;
And though it's reigned for far too long,
It too shall surely die!

So let us all with cheerful hearts
Be free from anxious gloom;
Let's set our minds on Christ above,
And on His empty tomb!

Let's think on heaven's blissful joy,
And on the death of death;
For that shall be our blessed hope,
When draws our final breath!

Can be sung to the tune of "All Hail the Power of Jesus' Name" (CORONA-TION) or "Auld Lang Syne" (without the chorus)

The Grace of God, So Vast and Free

The grace of God, so vast and free,
The cross of Christ displayed.
Atop the hill of Calvary,
The debt of sin was paid.

God's grace shall meet my ev'ry need,
And bring my heart good cheer.
From death and hell I have been freed,
So what have I to fear?

God's grace, my only hope in life,
My only hope in death;
I'll cling to grace in ev'ry strife,
And 'till my final breath.

The grace of God shall be my theme
Until the day I die;
And even then my heart will sing
Of boundless grace on high.

Can be sung to the tune of "Amazing Grace" (NEW BRITAIN) or "Jerusalem, My Happy Home" (LAND OF REST)

By Faith

By faith I look to Christ my Lord,
Who paid the debt I'd ne'er afford;
I look beyond myself to see
The One whose blood shall plead for me.

By faith I daily fly to Thee,
The spotless Lamb of Calvary;
Who took my sins and bore them all,
Redeeming me from Adam's fall.

By faith I trust in God's own Son,
And humbly plead what He has done;
I run to Christ my Savior's side,
Believing 'twas for me He died.

By faith I rest assured and free;
The risen Lord now speaks for me.
What charge to me can e'er be laid,
Since Jesus has atonement made?

By faith I'll enter heaven's joy,
Receiving sight to there employ;
And when I see Him face to face,
I'll truly know His saving grace!

Can be sung to the tune of "Praise God from Whom All Blessings Flow" (OLD 100TH) or "Jesus Shall Reign" (DUKE STREET)

What Hope Have We, Before Our God?

What hope have we, before our God,
Knowing our wretched, sinful state?
Perfection is His meas'ring rod,
And all we have is what He hates.

No righteousness to call our own,
Nothing but filthy rags to boast;
But trusting in Christ's work alone,
He saves us to the uttermost.

Our only hope, we do confess:
Jesus the Christ died in our place.
Now He supplies our righteousness,
Redeeming us from Adam's race.

Now in our ears the gospel rings;
It's drowning out our guilt and shame.
And to our hearts the Spirit brings
Pardon for sin in Jesus' name.

In Christ alone we're justified,
Shielded from wrath by nail-scarred hands;
His cross provides a place to hide,
And a sure hope in which to stand.

Can be sung to the tune of "When I Survey the Wondrous Cross" (HAMBURG)

To Christ My Praise Shall Ever Be

To Christ my praise shall ever be,
For by His blood He rescued me
From sin's accursed, wretched spell,
And from the grips of death and hell.

My sin incurred a hopeless debt,
But Christ has all my payment met.
By Jesus' blood I've been set free;
To Him my praise shall ever be.

It was my cross that Christ did bear,
And mine the sin that sent Him there.
And still He suffered willingly;
To Him my praise shall ever be.

How oft sin's damning voice is heard,
But Jesus speaks a better word.
His blood assures and comforts me;
To Him my praise shall ever be.

You fleshly passions, which I fight,
You chains of sin, which hold me tight;
From you one day I will be free
To praise my Lord more perfectly!

And when His lovely face I see,
The Lamb of God who died for me,
My lips shall sing repeatedly:
To Christ my praise shall ever be!

Can be sung to the tune of "Though I May Speak with Bravest Fire" (GIFT OF LOVE) or "Higher Ground" (HIGHER GROUND) without the refrain

Sweet, Melodious Praise

In honor of Ronald E. Boud

Creation sings its Maker's praise,
And echoes all around;
Its songs pour forth in countless ways,
In symphonies of sound.

Let us whom Christ by blood redeemed
Sound forth our praises too;
For we've more reason to esteem
The songs our God is due.

So let our music ring with joy,
Let ev'ry note be praise;
No greater theme can songs employ
Than God's redeeming grace.

Now tune we all our joyous cries
Into one grateful song;
And let our voices harmonize
With music loud and strong.

And oh, the music that abounds
When sinners saved rejoice,
When ev'ry instrument resounds
In union with each voice.

Now may our God be glorified
As we our voices raise;
May He receive this swelling tide
Of sweet, melod'ous praise.

Can be sung to the tune of "O for a Thousand Tongues" (AZMON)

Sinners' Never-Ceasing Praise

O Christ, our true and living Head,
Our Savior and our God;
You suffered in the sinner's stead,
And bought us with Your blood.
What tribute fits this blood-bought grace,
But sinners' never-ceasing praise?

Your precious blood has washed away
The stain of guilt and sin;
Now Satan's left with naught to say,
And we have peace within.
What tribute fits this pard'ning grace,
But sinners' never-ceasing praise?

Though holy wrath was once our dread,
Our punishment You bore;
Because Your sinless blood was shed,
God's wrath we dread no more!
What tribute fits this matchless grace,
But sinners' never-ceasing praise?

This saving act of Triune love,
Achieved by God the Son,
Gives substance to the songs above,
Sung to the Three in One.
What tribute fits this saving grace,
But sinners' never-ceasing praise?

Salvation's Tolling Bell

For the 2013 annual gathering of the Tennessee Baptist Convention in Chattanooga, in which a "Salvation Bell" was emphasized

'Twas grace that tuned my ears to hear
Salvation's tolling bell;
How sweet it sounded in my ears,
And sweet its echo still.

But how I long to hear it more,
That sweet, salvation bell;
To hear it ring from shore to shore,
The gospel's triumph tell.

So let me share with ev'ry soul
The news that Jesus saves;
Then let that bell begin to toll,
And sound the Savior's praise.

Oh, let a harvest of the lost
Be saved and gathered in;
And let the glories of the cross
Ring o'er and o'er again.

Oh, let that bell ring loud and strong,
Oh, let its ringing swell;
And let it raise a vict'ry song
That shakes the gates of hell.

Can be sung to the tune of "Amazing Grace" (NEW BRITAIN)

Jesus, Jesus, Faithful Friend

For my children

Jesus, Jesus, faithful Friend,
Died to save us from our sin.
How we thank You for Your grace,
For Your suff'ring in our place.
Jesus, thank You for the cross,
For Your love, and what it cost.

Jesus, Jesus, faithful Friend,
Though You died, You rose again.
Though our curse You fully bore,
Now You live forevermore.
Jesus, Jesus, Savior, Friend,
Praise to You shall never end.

Can be sung to the tune of "Twinkle, Twinkle, Little Star"

Lord Most High, Show Me Love

Lord above, Lord Most High,

Show me love; hear my cry:

I have sinned; I was wrong; I repent.

Through Your Son, whom You sent, please forgive all my sin.

Hear my cry, Lord above, show me love.

Can be sung to the tune of "Precious Lord, Take My Hand" (PRECIOUS LORD)

Baptized in Union with Our Lord

For Ella, on her baptism

We were buried therefore with him by baptism into death, in order that, just as Christ was raised from the dead by the glory of the Father, we too might walk in newness of life. (Romans 6:4)

Baptized in union with our Lord,
Like Him we're called to die;
Those waters are to us a cross,
Where sin is crucified.

Baptized in union with our Lord,
Those waters, like a grave,
Are where our old and sinful selves
Get buried 'neath the wave.

Baptized in union with our Lord,
Rejoice that it is true:
That from those waters, just like Christ,
We're raised to life anew!

Baptized and raised, as though reborn,
Alive to God above;
The Father's pleased to call us sons;
In Christ, we are belov'd.

Baptized according to the Word,
And in the threefold name;
Our faith in Father, Spirit, Son,
We do hereby proclaim.

Can be sung to the tune of "O God, Our Help in Ages Past" (ST. ANNE)

The Word of God Shall Ever Stand

The grass withers, the flower fades, but the word of our God will stand forever. (Isaiah 40:8)

The Word of God shall ever stand,
Though we like flowers fade.
So on God's Word we shall depend;
Our minds shall there be stayed.

The Word of God shall ever stand,
Though foes and fears arise;
Our sword and shield, it shall defend
Against the Tempter's lies.

The Word of God shall ever stand,
No promise ever fail.
It has, it must, it will withstand
The very gates of hell.

The Word of God shall ever stand;
Its truth shall never wane.
Amid the shifting, sinking sands,
Our refuge it remains.

The Word of God shall ever stand,
Our true and trusted guide,
To lead us to that Promised Land
Where peace and rest abide.

Can be sung to the tune of "O God, Our Help in Ages Past" (ST. ANNE)

What Joy to Know the One True God

But now that you have come to know God, or rather to be known by God . . . (Galatians 4:9)

What joy to know the one true God,
Jehovah is His name;
And know His Son, whose precious blood
Does save from sin and shame.
What joy to know the sovereign God,
Who calms the raging sea;
To know He's working for my good,
And that He cares for me.

How great to know this King divine,
Enthroned in majesty.
But greater still, what joy is mine
To know that He knows me!
I scarce can fathom that it's true,
It's hard to think it so;
That I—a sinner, through and through—
Am God's delight to know.

But yes, 'tis true, I'm known on high
By God who reigns above;
I am the apple of His eye,
The object of His love.
The King of kings unrivaled stands,
Yet He gives thought to me;
My name He's graven on His hands,
And His I'll ever be.

So when my doubting, fearful soul
Is tempted to despair,
I'll trust my faithful Shepherd's hold,
And rest within His care.
I'll trust that He is always good,
And claim with certainty
That though I may forget my God,
He'll never forget me!

Can be sung to the tune of "I Sing the Mighty Power of God" (FOREST GREEN)

Christ Has Saved Us, Christ Alone

Lift your voices, let us sing
Praises to our gracious King.
From His Spirit to our hearts,
Sweet assurance He imparts.
Christ has saved us, Christ alone;
By His blood, our sin's atoned.

No more fear and no more shame,
Satan's lies are all the same.
If the guilt of sin delay,
With assurance, we can say:
Christ has saved us, Christ alone;
By His blood, our sin's atoned.

Words alone cannot explain
Love that cleansed our crimson stain.
Nor our minds e'er comprehend
Grace that pardoned all our sin.
Christ has saved us, Christ alone;
By his blood, our sin's atoned.

When no more this life we see,
Then in heaven we shall be.
There we'll join the countless host,
And still this shall be our boast:
Christ has saved us, Christ alone;
By His blood, our sin's atoned.

Can be sung to the tune of "Rock of Ages, Cleft for Me" (TOPLADY)

O Sing of Christ, My Savior, Sing

How foul and full of sin am I,
And wedded to my lusts;
For when the devil tells me lies,
His words I'm prone to trust.
His ev'ry damning, wicked word,
I'm tempted to believe;
Until by grace the gospel's heard,
And then my soul's relieved.

Refrain:
O sing of Christ, my Savior, sing,
And let the gospel loudly ring!
O sing of Christ, my Savior, sing,
My gracious God, my Priest and King.

So let the devil roar with lies,
Condemn me to my face;
'Cause there's a truth he can't deny,
A great exchange by grace—
Where Christ has taken all my sin,
And bore it on the tree;
And all His righteousness has been
Imputed free to me.

And when before that great white throne,
In judgment I shall stand;
I'll trust in Christ and Him alone,
Who met the Law's demands.
And though the devil may accuse,
His ploys will be denied;
For I shall plead the blood-bought news
Of Christ the crucified!

Additional Stanza of "Holy, Holy, Holy"

To be sung between the 3rd and 4th existing stanzas

Holy, holy, holy, raise our eyes to Calv'ry,
That we might behold Thy Son condemned upon the tree.
Oh, how sin has cost Thee! Oh, Thy grace and mercy!
Christ fully punished; sinners fully free.

Additional Stanza of "He Will Hold Me Fast"

To be sung between the 1st and 2nd existing stanzas

Through each dark night of my soul,
Christ will hold me fast.
This one truth my fears control:
He will hold me fast.
When I feel I've hope no more,
I recall the past;
How my God's proved o'er and o'er:
He will hold me fast.

Additional Stanza of
"Mine Eyes Have Seen the Glory"

To be sung between the 4th and 5th existing stanzas

I have read the gospel's triumph
Writ in love on Calv'ry's hill,
How our greatest foes were conquered
By the blood that Jesus spilled;
How the promised seed of woman
Crushed the serpent 'neath His heel.
Our God is marching on.

Additional Stanza of "The Church's One Foundation"

To be sung between the 2nd and 3rd existing stanzas

With sin's deadly deception,
And tendency to blind,
She must pursue correction
Among her own some time.
In this she takes no pleasure;
It fills her heart with woe.
But she must take such measures,
For love compels her so.

Additional Stanza of "Our Great God"

To be sung between the 2nd and 3rd existing stanzas

Lord, when we're sinking 'neath the load
Of sin and guilt and shame,
Remind our fearful, doubting hearts
Just why our Savior came.

He came to bear our dreadful curse,
And from it set us free.
So help us see our sin and shame
Nailed fast to Calv'ry's tree!

Poems

Artists

Good artists, whether they be
poets or painters, musicians or novelists,
see the same things everyone else sees.
Only, the artists look longer,
and from different angles.
They stop and stare;
they linger and ponder,
refusing to be bored or unaffected.
Then they tell us what they've seen.
And it turns out to be
exactly what we should have seen,
if only we had taken the time.

Shared Wonder

The art we most enjoy—
whether stories or sketches,
paintings or poems,
music or movies,
sermons or songs—
is the fruit of private wonder
being made public.
The end result of art, then,
is shared wonder.
It says, "Join me.
Look with me.
Let's marvel and weep
and wonder together."

How Writers Write

Stories are born
while watching the world
in wide-eyed wonder.
He who has eyes to see,
let him see.

Maternity

For Anna, on her first Mother's Day

How wonderfully marvelous
(yet altogether natural)
has been the transformation of my wife
into motherhood.
It's amazing how quickly she mastered
the mundane matters of maternity,
and turned them into something
truly beautiful to behold.
I sometimes pause (without her knowledge)
and listen in as she reads or sings to our daughter.
I'm tempted to cry, but I don't—
because my smiling prevents it.

A Little Mirror of My Own Depravity

How humbling it is
to see my own depravity—
my own stubborn defiance
toward You, O Lord—
reflected back to me
in the defiance of my child.
What patience You have!
And what fools we are!

Truly, how foolish of me
to think that You have anything
but my best interests at heart.
All my rebellion is but
ignorance and unbelief—
ignorance of Your wisdom
and a lack of trust
in Your steadfast goodness.

Grown Man Crying

I saw a grown man cry today,
but I didn't pity him.
I admired him,
because he cared so deeply
about something (or someone)
that it moved him to tears.
Oh, that more grown men would cry
over meaningful things.

Motherhood Briefly Summarized

For Anna, on Mother's Day

Anticipation . . . experienced.
Pain . . . endured.
Sacrifices . . . made.
Sleep . . . lost.
Diapers . . . changed.
Clothes . . . washed.
Meals . . . prepared.
Laughter . . . shared.
Tears . . . shed.
Medicine . . . administered.
Band-aids . . . applied.
Hugs . . . enjoyed.
Kisses . . . given.
Worry . . . felt.
Stories . . . told.
Truth . . . taught.
Books . . . read.
Hymns . . . sung.
Prayers . . . offered.
Example . . . set.
Nurture . . . provided.
Love . . . demonstrated.
Joy . . . known.
Husband . . . grateful.
Children . . . blessed.

This Verbal Tribute We Now Raise

For Anna, on behalf of our children

For all the toil and all the tears,
for countless pray'rs and list'ning ears,
for ev'ry long and sleepless night,
for finding joy in our delight;
for words of wisdom that you share,
for all the hats you're made to wear,
for sacrificing time and health,
for always giving of yourself;
for ev'ry burden that you bear,
for all the ways you show you care,
for ev'ry kind and thoughtful deed,
for all you do that we don't see;
for untold blessings still in store,
for all these things and so much more,
we find it hard to rightly show
the love you're due, the thanks we owe.
So as an effort of our praise,
this verbal tribute we now raise.
It's so much less than you deserve,
this meager monument of words,
but here it stands to honor you,
a symbol of our gratitude,
a way for us to somehow say:
We thank you, Mom, this Mother's Day!

Simple Pleasures?

They say, "Simple minds
have simple pleasures."
And they may be right.
But I'd prefer to think
that I take pleasure
in the profundity of simple things.

Of course, that might just be
because I'm too simple-minded
to know the difference.

Conversation as Transformation

A good friend called me on the phone,
but I hadn't the time to call him back.
I had a number of things to do that day,
and that wasn't on my list.
But out of courtesy,
and in honor of our long friendship,
and trusting that our conversation would be brief,
I dialed his number.
An hour later, I hung up the phone,
completely forgetting my previous duties
that had seemed so important.
Shared memories, laughter,
the joy of friendship—
that's what mattered now.
The grace of God, extended through conversation,
turned this dreary Winter day
into a beautiful Spring morning.

On Poetry

Have you ever noticed
that when people want to say something significant,
something memorable, something striking,
they reach for poetry rather than prose?

Think of life's most meaningful moments—
graduations, weddings, funerals.
Think of history's most stirring speeches—
political, religious, dramatic.
What do most of these hold in common?

The presence of poetry.

Music and Memory

The relationship between music
and memory is a mystery,
but a mystery common to all men.
Who among us hasn't heard a song
and instantly remembered a person
or a place or a season of life?
Even if that particular person or place
or that time of life was a distant,
even forgotten, memory,
music has a mysterious way
of making it feel like only yesterday.
Memories always hitch rides on melodies.
It's as if music is some sort of melodious key
that unlocks men's memories.
Of course, some of those memories
we'd rather remain hidden and locked away,
but music and memory, it seems,
have minds of their own.

The Mercy of the Mundane

Lord, help me see
the beauty in monotony;
help me relish in the mercy
of mundane moments;
and help me rejoice in the regular,
to find joy in the ordinary.

Silence Has a Voice

Silence has a voice.
Sometimes it whispers;
sometimes it roars.
It can sound like snow,
or it can sound like thunder.
But make no mistake,
it speaks—speaks to those
who have the ears to hear.
Shhh! Can you hear it?

Shade Trees Need Roots

To enjoy the benefits of the shade
requires patience
for the roots to sink down deep
and the tree to grow.

Problem is, we want the benefits
without the patience.
We want the shade
without the roots.

The all-pervasive immediacy of our age
has left us wanting
long-term results
through short-term effort.

We like to measure growth in seconds,
and nanoseconds,
rather than years and decades.

Lord, Break the Silence Long Endured

Advent

Lord, break the silence long endured,
and end the darkened night;
let anxious fears all rest assured
with news of coming light.

O how we need to hear Your voice,
the good news that You bring;
good news in which we can rejoice,
the coming of our King.

Let prophets' words be now fulfilled
in all their grand design;
and mysteries be now revealed
through grace and pow'r divine.

The second Adam, send to us,
redeem our fallen race;
Immanuel, great God with us,
come quickly with Your grace.

The Prophets' Single Note

Advent

Let loose your tongues, ye men of old
as once you did with Israel.
And tell again what must be told—
the story of Immanuel.

O prophets' words which have grown dim,
shine forth again with heat and light.
Proclaim to us the words of Him
who'll free us from our sinful plight.

Now give us ear and we shall speak
the message that you long to hear.
For if it's Jesus that you seek,
then we have spoken loud and clear.

Behold, the virgin shall conceive
and bear a son for David's line.
A special name He shall receive,
for 'twas Isaiah's telling sign.

He shall be called Immanuel,
yes, "God with us" shall be His name.
The deepest darkness He'll dispel,
with light divine in humble frame.

This Mighty God, this Prince of Peace,
will ever sit on David's throne.
His righteous reign shall never cease,
and all will bow to Him alone.

This King shall come from Bethlehem,
our brother Micah did foretell.
A ruler for the sons of men,
a shepherd over Israel.

This object of the devil's scorn
shall come to you in joy sublime.
The Son of God by virgin born,
He shall arrive in perfect time.

So wait for Him as once did we,
with longing hearts and watchful eyes.
Yes, Jesus Christ will come to thee,
so don't believe the scoffers' lies.

The world's deceit we'll not esteem.
No, we shall hope and watch and pray.
In God we'll trust, though all may seem
to contradict what you doth say.

Your words have come to cheer and bless
our ever-longing, searching hearts.
And this they've done we must confess,
providing comfort from the start.

So thank you for your faithfulness
in sounding forth that single note,
whose joyful sound, we can attest
is found in ev'ry word you wrote.

That single note of Christ we've heard;
within our hearts it strikes a chord.
It sings of the incarnate Word,
and tells of our eternal Lord.

So with you now that note we raise,
and join the hopeful proclamation.
Our coming Lord demands our praise,
He is our hope and our salvation.

A Symphony of Sweet Delight

Advent

Sound the notes that heaven hears,
and let them ring in sinners' ears.
Sing the chorus sung above
that echoes forth redeeming love.

Angels, join in harmony
to make a joyous melody.
Silence all the noise of sin,
and let God's symphony begin.

Strike the prophets' hopeful chord,
and listen for the coming Lord.
Run the bow across their strings,
and hear their songs to Christ the King.

Ring the bells of virgin-birth!
Glory to God and peace on earth!
Like the shepherds, spread the word,
and let the angels' news be heard.

Christ has come in grace divine,
a son in David's royal line.
Born in David's Bethlehem,
and born to free us from our sin.

Christ has come! Rejoice, rejoice!
Now's the time to lift your voice,
and join with ev'ry tribe and race
in songs of God's redeeming grace.

Ev'ry bar and ev'ry measure
speaks of our abiding Treasure:
Jesus, our Immanuel,
who saves us from despair and hell.

Blow the horn of hope and peace!
The gospel sings of our release
from Satan's damning, sinful ploys,
and all his wicked, evil noise.

Hear the gospel music play,
and let the Spirit have His way.
Let symphonic sounds impart,
to quicken ev'ry lifeless heart.

Feel the rhythm, hear the sounds,
when mercy sings and grace abounds.
Oh! the joyous orchestration,
freeing us from condemnation.

Christ has come, and this we know,
a gracious gift He did bestow:
A symphony of sweet delight,
where ev'ry note is played just right.

And oh! the joy to be displayed
when this, the final note, is played:
Sound the trumpet; let it blast,
for Christ's return has come at last!

Christmas Is a Canvas

Christmas, it seems,
is a canvas on which God
delights to dazzle us
with displays of divine mystery.

Manly Tears

There's no shame in a man crying.
In fact, there are times
when it's a shame for a man not to cry.
There *is* shame, though,
in the man who has no good reasons
for which to cry.

Anxiety

I received a phone call this morning
that's made me anxious all the day.
The outcome's out of my control,
but that's certainly not stopped me
from being consumed with wondering
and fearing and hoping what it will be.
At the heart of the matter is the glaring fact
that in my heart I don't trust the matter
to a God who promises good for me.
I care far too much about my anxieties,
not nearly enough about casting those cares
on the only One who truly cares for me.
My anxiety is really self-sufficiency,
disguising itself as something else, something less.

Take Me to Gethsemane

Oh, take me to Gethsemane,
that hallowed garden space;
where Christ my Lord, in agony,
has fallen on His face.

Take me there, in heart and mind,
within Gethsemane;
wonders there my soul shall find,
and myst'ries surely see.

Oh, take me to Gethsemane,
that Eden in reverse;
the second Adam there I see,
and in His cup my curse.

Oh, the depths of Jesus' woes
in dark Gethsemane;
as His full ob'dience grows,
so too, His agony.

Enduring the Wilderness

It should come as no surprise
that our earthly pilgrimage
is often compared
to the wilderness experience
of the Israelites.
Nor is it by accident
that the English word *wilderness*
contains the word *wild* within it.
The wilderness is anything but safe or tame.
It contains many dangers, toils, and snares.
But it's also the only sure path
to the Promised Land.
And thankfully, that path
is well worn by the pilgrims
who've gone before us,
and, more importantly,
by our Lord, who first cleared the path.

Resurrecting Ebenezer

Then Samuel took a stone and set it up between Mizpah and Shen and called its name Ebenezer; for he said, "Till now the LORD has helped us." (1 Samuel 7:12)

"Here I raise mine Ebenezer, hither by Thy help I'm come . . ."
—Robert Robinson

My Ebenezer's fallen;
my "stone of help"
no longer stands.
Mercy's marker,
once looming tall,
now lies forgotten,
overgrown and abandoned.

But fallen stones,
like lifeless bones,
can be raised again.
So resurrect this Ebenezer
in my heart and mind,
and let it stand for all to see,
a monument to grace.

Winter in My Soul

Exactly how, I'm not quite sure;
I know only that it came.
Depression knocked upon the door,
and it seemed to know my name.

Soon its sorrows stormed my castle,
plundering my peace and pride.
Fighting wasn't worth the hassle,
so I closed myself inside.

Discouragement began to rise;
discontentment dug in deep.
I knew the truth but, still, the lies
just kept playing on repeat.

Shadows settled all around me.
Darkness fell to cloud my view.
Joy seemed like a distant mem'ry;
all my hope felt hollow too.

The growing darkness took its toll;
the light grew dim around me.
It felt like Winter in my soul,
and Spring was slow to find me.

A Mid-March Musing

Spring is at the door,
the Winter almost gone;
flowers bloom once more,
and birds take up their song.

Landscapes drab and drear
now burst with colors bright;
life from death appears,
and beauty from the blight.

Still, the ancient curse
fights hard to hold its sway;
yet signs of its reverse
point to a better day.

Yes, each new Spring foretells
a promise sure and true:
The King creation hails
is making all things new.

An Ode to My First Love

When the grass turns green and temperatures rise,
and Old Man Winter has said his goodbyes;
when daylight lengthens to shorten the night,
and mem'ries emerge of boyhood delight;
when Spring's in the air with blue skies above
my heart's drawn again to its first true love . . .
baseball!

At the Corner of Clark and Addison

In honor of the one-hundredth anniversary of Wrigley Field

At the corner of Clark and Addison
stands one of the world's most precious diamonds,
the crown jewel of the Chicago Cubs.

With its bright, beckoning marquee,
its iconic ivy and rustic, red brick,
its historic centerfield scoreboard
and quaint neighborhood surroundings,
its sounds of organ music and seventh-inning singing,
its day games and bleacher seats,
Wrigley Field leaves an indelible impression
on the hearts of players and fans alike.

It remains, even after a century,
a living landmark, occupying
some of baseball's most sacred space.
If baseball is a part of American civil religion,
then this is surely one of its finest sanctuaries,
a grand cathedral of American culture and sport
(though it must be said that the prayers of its faithful attenders
too often go unanswered!).

Over the years, Cubs fans have been subjected
to a lot of ugly baseball, but let it be said
that never has baseball been played
in a more beautiful setting
than the "Friendly Confines" of Wrigley Field.

Death Brings Resurrection

The fallen leaves
from autumn trees
descend to their earthly tomb;
yet limbs which shed
their leaves all dead
trust new life again will bloom.

'Cause little mounds
of lifeless browns
are only half the story;
for lively green
will soon be seen
with Spring and all its glory.

'Tis all a sign
of truth divine
revealed for our reflection;
as one life ends,
a new begins—
yes, death brings resurrection.

As I Looked Out at the Sea

As I looked out at the sea,
a thought came to me suddenly—
Noah saw the same as me,
and Jesus too in Galilee.
These waves, which crash consistently
o'er time and down through history,
are filled with untold mystery.
And if you listen carefully,
you'll hear their Maker's majesty.

Strangely Beautiful Grace

Most of the time, a meal is just a meal.
It satisfies the appetite.
And there's nothing wrong with that.
But on rare occasions,
it is so much more.
Not necessarily because of the food,
but because of something else—
because of the person sitting across from you,
and the conversation that ensues.
I had such a meal today.
The food—cheap.
The atmosphere—lacking.
But the company, the conversation—
like a delicacy to be slowly savored;
to waste or rush a single word
would have been shameful,
would have been inconsiderate.
It's not that we solved
the problems of the world;
we didn't even solve our own
plethora of problems.
But we shared life—
pains, struggles, joys—
and there was something
strangely beautiful about it.
Grace seems to work that way.
It's beautiful but strangely so,
like a messy masterpiece.

And Such Is the Grace of God

I'm amazed (though not often enough)
at the beauty that comes out of brokenness,
whether it's beautiful music birthed out of misery
or beautiful poetry inspired by pain.
One person's hurt produces another person's healing.
And such is the grace of God.

Grace and Gravity

Grace and gravity,
both of them forces
far beyond our control.
Grace and gravity,
both of them laws
learned through pain.
Grace and gravity,
both of them instruments
employed by God,
but in very different ways.

Gravity pulls us,
always downward.
Grace, it lifts us,
always heavenward.
Gravity says,
"What goes up
must come down."
But grace says,
"Who falls down
must be lifted up."

Gravity seems
to work against us.
But grace is always
working for us.
Gravity's a force
we like to defy.
But grace is a gift,
a wonderful gift,
in which we ever
only want to delight.

Prayer Pondered

The vivid verbs of prayer:
yearning, longing,
hungering, thirsting,
asking, seeking,
beseeching, pleading,
needing, crying out;
along with the emotive actions of prayer:
weeping, wailing,
kneeling, bowing,
silence, shouting,
beating our breast,
and clinching our fists;
should teach us all a truth about prayer—
it's humility in action,
evidence of our own inadequacy.
Prayer reveals our weakness,
but it magnifies God's strength.
It's the most earnest expression
of our faith and dependence.
We are poor beggars, 'tis true,
but riches untold are at our disposal.
So keep longing, keep yearning,
keep trusting, keep crying.
Child of God, you're not an orphan.
Your Father hears you, and He will answer.

A Pilgrim Prayer

We pray to You, Three-Person God,
as we on life's journey trod.
All the while, we look to Thee,
faithful trav'lers help us be.

Both our journey's Source and End,
our broken lives are Yours to mend.
'Cause if we pilgrims must be honest,
we rarely seem to make much progress.

We persevere each trying hour,
leaning on Thy sovereign power.
While on this pathway You have made,
see us on by love's strong aide.

Wrong we are to walk alone,
or face this journey on our own.
The Church, our burdens they do share,
and keep us from such great despair.

On Thy Word revealed we stand,
until we reach that Promised Land.
Let Thy Spirit be our guide,
till in Thy presence we abide.

An Indictment on Evangelical Worship

Set the stage and dim the lights;
create my mood with sounds and sights.
Out-do all you did last week,
and never let the silence speak.
Entertain me at all costs;
blur the lines 'tween true and false.
Smile and tell me all's okay,
I'll believe whate'er you say.
Give me mirrors; give me smoke;
fill me with clichés and jokes.

Like an orphan with no story,
cut me off from all before me.
Hide the pain and fake the smile;
lamentation's out of style.
Give me milk and warm the bottle;
make sure it's the latest model.
Numb my mind with borrowed tricks;
feed my soul with Pixy Stix.
Don't confront what lurks within,
or else I'll never come again.

Preaching Is Preceded by Listening

In honor of my preaching professor, Dr. Robert Smith Jr.

Much more is learned by listening
than by talking;
from open ears
rather than an open mouth.
In fact, it ought to be a rule
(and a rule which we should follow)
that speaking be preceded
by attentive listening.
Anything significant
that ever has been said
(or that ever will be said)
is the fruit of much listening.
And preaching is no different.

Good preaching is the product
of good listening—
to God and to His Word.
We preachers sit before an open Bible,
listening—listening for God to speak
what He has already spoken.
Then, and only then,
do we stand before His people
and open our mouths.
We speak, but only
because we first have listened.
And our listening
qualifies us to speak.

New Morning Mercies

The steadfast love of the LORD never ceases;
his mercies never come to an end;
they are new every morning;
great is your faithfulness. (Lamentations 3:22–23)

Morning mercies, without fail,
awaken me each day;
fresh arriving, never stale,
and never with delay.

How faithfully they're given
from God, who reigns on high;
like manna sent from heaven,
each day a new supply.

The Joyous Song of Mercy

Naked in our sin and shame,
like Adam, let us hide;
how we fear Mt. Sinai's flame.
Oh! will it e'er subside?

Frightful, guilty, here we stand,
the dread too much to bear;
the holy law's strict demands
have caused us this despair.

Does any hope now remain,
and where can it be found?
Is there not some sweet refrain
in which God's grace abounds?

There is! There is! Mercy sings,
and oh! its joyous song.
Hear the gracious news it brings;
its voice is loud and strong.

It speaks about the sinless One,
who came and took our place;
God the Father's only Son,
who purchased saving grace.

Jesus Christ, His precious name,
oh! let it now resound;
He, our Savior, bore our shame,
and wore our guilty crown.

This is why the Son was sent,
and followed Calv'ry's path;
to receive our punishment,
and bear the Father's wrath.

Christ has quenched Mt. Sinai's flame;
its dreaded curse He bore.
He's removed our guilt and shame;
they're gone forevermore!

We've been pardoned by His blood;
in Christ we're justified;
mercy flowing like a flood
has justice satisfied.

Let us no more naked hide,
or fear the law's demands;
Jesus suffered, bled, and died
that we might righteous stand.

Clothed with Jesus' righteousness,
adorned in Him alone;
all His merit we possess
as if it was our own.

God condemned His only Son
that we'd be counted free;
'tis love to ne'er be outdone,
and grace beyond degree!

I Once Was Dead in Sin and Strife

I once was dead in sin and strife,
and knew no will but mine;
but God has quickened me to life
by sovereign grace divine!

To base desires I was a slave,
and under their control;
but Jesus Christ is strong to save;
He freed my shackled soul!

Although my heart was hard as stone,
and vile with ev'ry beat;
for all my sins Christ has atoned,
in Him I stand complete!

My blinded eyes were shut by sin,
the dark my only sight;
but God, in mercy, opened them,
and flooded me with light!

My lifeless tongue was resting lame,
no words my mouth could bring;
till on my lips God put His name,
and loosed my tongue to sing!

And sing I shall to Christ my King,
my Savior and my God;
loud praises I will ever bring.
I'll glory in His blood!

And when from earth I shall depart,
and when it's time to die;
I'll join the saints and sing my part
in songs of praise on high!

True Repentance and Contrition

True repentance and contrition,
these are our desp'rate need;
help us see our ill condition
in ev'ry sinful deed.

Reveal to us our heinous crimes,
our vile and wretched hearts,
and how we've spurned a thousand times
the good Your Law imparts.

Let us fear Thy righteous anger,
that awful, holy wrath;
cause our hearts to feel the danger
which haunts the crooked path.

But please remind us, and with haste,
of Christ, the sinner's friend;
and preach to us of gospel grace,
of pardon from our sin.

Assure us, Lord, that You are good;
remind us of Your love,
that Christ redeemed us by His blood,
and pleads for us above.

Now help us daily die to sin,
the Spirit as our aide;
and rid us of what dwells within,
until like Christ we're made.

Theological Antonyms

The opposite of religious hubris
is gospel humility.

Religious hubris breeds superiority
on the grounds of moral performance.
But it's a misplaced superiority,
because it's built on a lie.
All who gather on those grounds
will surely fall.

Gospel humility yields unity
at the foot of the cross.
And it's an appropriate unity,
because it's built on the truth.
All who gather there
stand on a sure and firm foundation.

Religious hubris
sees no need for a Savior.
Gospel humility
sees not only the need for a Savior,
but the Savior Himself,
meeting that very need.

Religious hubris stands tall,
but will one day be brought low.
Gospel humility bows low,
but will one day be exalted.

Liquid Love

Jesus' blood is liquid love.

The sweat of Gethsemane,
the wounds of Calvary,
the cup of Communion—

all are liquid love.

The Living Need the Dying

The living need the dying,
not so much as a reminder of death,
but as a reminder of life.

The Earthly End of a Life Well Lived

For Bobby Newton

The earthly end
of a life well lived
should, in my opinion,
be marked by both
tears and smiles.

Indeed, one mark
of a beloved man must surely be
that the sounds heard at his funeral
are a mixture of crying and laughing.

Crying,
because he will most certainly be missed.
And laughing,
because he is remembered so fondly.

I know that's why I've shed tears today.
But it's also why I'm smiling,
even as I wipe away the tears.

So farewell, my friend,
until we meet again
in that place where all our crying
will be turned to laughing.

Strangely Familiar

If I must die, and die I must,
son of Adam that I am,
and if my death is not untimely
or unexpected,
then, if it can be arranged,
and it's not too much trouble,
let it be in a familiar place,
surrounded by familiar people,
singing familiar hymns,
and reading familiar promises
from that most familiar of Books;
because though I've never been there,
I believe I'll find the Celestial City
somehow strangely familiar.

Resurrection Morning
(or The Very First Easter)

The darkness turns to morning,
and Hell's caught by surprise.
The corpse it had been taunting
just opened up His eyes.

That borrowed tomb's now empty.
Its stone's been rolled away.
Its occupant from Galilee
booked just a 2-night stay.

Death itself has been defied;
in shame it hangs its head.
Jesus Christ the crucified
is risen from the dead!

www.ingramcontent.com/pod-product-compliance
Lightning Source LLC
Chambersburg PA
CBHW071054090426
42737CB00013B/2346